Where The Devil Lost His Boots

by
Kurt Lockhart

Table of Contents

Introduction   1

The Tireless Cyclist   3

The Amicable Authors   7

The Family Business   9

The Intrepid Entrepreneur   13

The Quintessential Gaúcho   15

From Club to Conservatory   17

At the Gym   19

The Bilingual Jokester   21

The Sunday Scaries   23

The Burger Joint   27

The Weekly Thud   29

The Devout Mathematician   33

The Dinner Party   35

The Expat Club   39

The English Enthusiast   41

The Wry Banker   43

The Brazilian Moon   47

Good Energy   49

Introduction

"There are no foreign lands. It is the traveler only who is foreign."

–Robert Louis Stevenson, *The Silverado Squatters*

I spent most of a year of my life living in Bagé, a Brazilian frontier town roughly halfway between Porto Alegre (the capital of the Brazilian state of Rio Grande do Sul) and Montevideo (the capital of Uruguay). It is a frontier town, a meeting place of Brazilian and Uruguayan culture. Because of its remoteness, locals often joke that it is "onde o diabo perdeu as botas" - where the devil lost his boots.

I grew up in Waco - a small town in the heart of Texas roughly halfway between Austin and Dallas. I went to Bagé looking for a change of pace, a window into a foreign culture, and an opportunity to enjoy new experiences. I found all of those things, but I also discovered so much that felt like home.

Bagé, like Waco, had a population of about 100,000, was halfway between two major cities, and was often looked down upon as dull or backwater or not having much to offer. If you drive out 30 miles from either Waco or Bagé, you might see similar sights - rolling, open plains with cows, horses and cowboys (gaúchos) dotting the horizon.

What do you do for fun when there aren't a multitude of big city options to entertain you? Wacoans and Bagéenses alike will watch sunsets, chat with their neighbors, and take the time to enjoy the simple pleasures of life. Maybe I have more in common with a Bagéense than I do with someone from Washington D.C, or New York City, and maybe they have more in common with me than they would with someone from São Paulo or Rio de Janeiro.

The stories in this book are my attempts to paint a picture of Bagé through conversations with the people who live there, to try to elicit what life is like, in their own words. Forgive my poor translation of most of these conversations from Portuguese to English.

To my fellow adventures, who, sight unseen, dared to spend many months of their lives in a small town in a remote part of a foreign land - thank you for sharing these moments with me. To the people living in Bagé who welcomed us with kindness, openness, and warmth - thank you for earnestly and honestly sharing your town and your stories. To the reader - I hope these stories show you a slice of life in a "foreign" land, and may this book take you on an extraordinary journey to where the devil lost his boots.

The Tireless Cyclist

"Do you want to stop for a Big Mac?" he teased, our bikes side by side as we pedaled up the hill. We were about two hours in on a bike ride down BR-473, the highway that connects Bagé to the Uruguayan border.

"You're starting to sound like an American…" I joked back at him, desperately yet cluelessly clicking gears on the bike in an attempt to ease my pain.

My main concern was this: I had no idea how much longer this ride would go. I had tried to ask him a couple minutes beforehand if we were halfway yet. He just chuckled. As is often the case when both people are not yet fully conversational in the other's language, I didn't know whether my question was truly understood. Did the laugh mean that we weren't even close to halfway, or was it just a friendly guess at an appropriate response to words he didn't know?

The cyclist and I met my first week in Bagé, when I was wandering around the city trying to get my bearings. He greeted me one morning when I walked into his shop, Tchê Gaúcho, which sells traditional clothing, decorations, and other items typical of the Brazilian state of Rio Grande do Sul. We got to talking, and I told him I was interested in getting a bike. He immediately dropped what he was doing, and gave me a ride to four different stores to compare various bike prices and styles. I've found this sort of radical hospitality and kindness – people going incredibly out of their way to help a stranger – very common during my time in Brazil.

I didn't end up buying a bike, but he offered to let me use one of his anytime I wanted to go for a ride. I took him up on his offer, and we met one Thursday morning at 9am at the Bagé airport. The airport was somewhat of a joke to the average Bagéense, because it did not offer commercial flights. It was mainly used by local horse breeders who are doing business in São Paulo.

"Here you go!" he said when I arrived, handing me a bag with professional racing clothes. I was touched to see he had even tucked a full water bottle in the road bike he had let me use.

"How'd you get started biking?" I asked, as we biked out of the airport parking lot and started out along the highway.

"About four years ago, I just decided to make this my thing. Now I bike every single day, except for Sundays. Normally I'll go with a friend or two, like yesterday we went to Aceguá and back."

I was flabbergasted by how casually he dropped this tidbit – that's an almost 80km roundtrip.

The highway south towards Uruguay is fairly flat, with beautiful vistas on each side full of lush fields, horses, and cows.

"Mmm, barbecue!" he said, pointing at a huge group of cows that had congregated right by the side of the road.

After about half an hour of riding, the sun was beating down and I was sweating profusely. I realized I have no idea how far we were going to go, and my legs were already starting to ache. I decided to chat a bit to keep my mind off it all.

"Do you think you'll ever leave Bagé?"

"Just for travel. My wife and I have two kids – a 3-year-old boy and a 17-year-old girl. If they move, we'll go visit them of course, but this is our home."

Towards the end of the ride, which was thankfully only a couple minutes after his Big Mac comment, he started singing "Eye of the Tiger" to encourage me. I couldn't help but laugh, and breathed a sigh of relief as I saw the airport appear around the next curve.

"I think I understand why this place is so dear to you. But what exactly is it about Rio Grande do Sul that you love so much?"

"Pride. People in Rio Grande do Sul are proud of where they are from, their culture, and their lifestyle. Most people in Brazil in general don't have a lot of national pride right now. Our country has a lot of problems, political and economic. People are doubting our institutions and are cynical about improvements in the future. But here, we know what we stand for and we are content with that."

The Amicable Authors

It was just a Facebook event in a language I was still trying to understand. Someone I had met briefly the week before had shared it, and from what I could translate, it was some sort of book launch. I showed up at the bookstore right at the time the event started. I walked into the back room, where a stack of books was sitting on the table, and only one person was there. It was a classic gringo move, arriving right on time. Everyone else knew to come half an hour late!

"Hello!" he said, shaking my hand warmly. "Glad you came!"

"Thanks! Can you tell me the story of this book?

"Sure! I'm working on getting authors together in the community. This book is a collection of poems and prose from over a dozen local folks. It's been hard, writers are a pretty reclusive bunch..."

"I can imagine. What kind of stuff do you write?"

He picked up a nearby book with a dragon on the cover. "This is the first novel in my fantasy series!"

"Incredible, congrats! Do you publish just in Brazil or are you hoping to distribute internationally?"

"No, I like it just in Brazil. It has Brazilian themes and slang that make it mainly relevant here."

Just then, about five other people showed up. I greeted all of them (a long process of many hugs and kisses), and it turned out that they were all the other writers of the book! I was the only fan who had showed up.

I was incredibly touched when, after just a few minutes of talking, they all signed the book and left individual notes for me. Here are my rough translations of a few:

"A very Brazilian hug for you! I hope that you have an incredible experience in Bagé."

"Life is made of moments, so live every second intensely."

"Words are more than they seem. They are inventions to try to define what we feel. It is an impossible thing to do, but we must continue trying..."

The Family Business

It all started our first weekend in town, when we were wandering around downtown Bagé, looking for a fun bar to hang out in.

We stopped for a moment in front of a huge mansion-esque building with the letters "JW" emblazoned on the outside. A group of people were sitting in the front lawn drinking and laughing, playing music, so I ventured in the open gate and said hello.

"Excuse me," I ask in Portuguese. "Is this a bar?"

One of the three men wearing jeans and blue button downs, each emblazoned with " JW", stood up and handed me a beer.

"No, but here's a drink!" he said.

"Oh, sorry!" I said, realizing my mistake. However, I still had no idea where we were. "We thought this was something else."

"No, stay! Have a seat, friends!" he said. "Where are you from?"

We got to talking with them, and realized that the three men in blue button downs were brothers who ran the business "JW" (where we were), which does car and property rentals and sales. JW is short for Jose Walter, their father who started the company.

Pretty soon, we were invited to their weekly Thursday pizza dinners at their office (definitely not a bar). We met the brothers' wives and kids, and got to know them better. They work very hard, 12 hours a day, along with their father, Jose Walter, and his wife. It was very inspiring to see this family that was so close, so successful, and also made time each week to really enjoy each other.

One Saturday morning at 8am, I was invited to give a lecture at their weekly company all-hands meeting on "American Culture". I found it difficult to encapsulate what that meant, and I ended up focusing on stereotypes many Brazilians have about us (everyone has lots of guns, lots of money, etc.) and of the many challenges facing the "American dream" (discrimination, inequality, etc.)

The next thing I know, after I finish, one of the brothers got up and gave a motivational speech:

"That's the kind of attitude you need to have, it will help you make sales! Be like him, be a go-getter, don't be afraid to make a relationship. Don't be afraid to make new friends even if it's not at a bar."

After the meeting, I was called into the office of JW himself. I was a bit nervous to be sitting in front of his desk, in the presence of such a powerful man. The office was full of huge legal books from his time as a lawyer, and the TV behind me blared Brazilian news commentary on recent American missile strikes on Syria. However, he warmly engaged me in small talk to ask about my experience so far in Brazil. Finally, he said,

"I've worked for many years building this business. It can be stressful at times, and I've put in many long hours. That's why I've recently picked up meditation."

He pulled out a book, and flipped a few pages to land on an article with his name on it.

"Here are my thoughts so far on it. I hope you enjoy it."

He scribbles an inscription inside the front cover, then pulls out an official looking seal and stamps just below.

"Don't be a stranger!" he says, and hands me the book.

The Intrepid Entrepreneur

In a rural Brazilian town of only about 100,000 people, there are over 10 different private, for-profit English schools. Some focus on teaching conjugation, while others emphasize conversation; some cater to children, while others focus on adults. However, not a single school in town has a native English speaker on staff.

Because of this, many schools reached out to Americans in town asking us to come to talk with their students. I happened to be walking around southern Bagé one day, and I spotted a shiny new building with a sign that said "Rockefeller Center". I decided to stop in and say hello.

"Let me show you around!" said the owner, and we walked upstairs to where the classrooms were. "We're very excited but nervous, because we open tomorrow!"

"Good luck! What inspired you to start an English school?"

"I used to teach at another school nearby, but it focused too much on grammar. I wanted this one to be more practical. I wanted to teach people how to have a conversation, how to put English to use rather than just memorize rules!"

"That makes sense. What else makes your school special?"

"We have a kitchen! Each week we have a day to practice cooking traditional foods from different English speaking areas. And we use it as a teaching opportunity to help people learn the language!"

"Ok, now I'm definitely coming back here often.."

"You're always welcome!"

The Quintessential Gaúcho

Almost every time I introduce myself in Bagé as a Texan, I hear a thrilling new stereotype about the state. Along with the typical references to religion, cowboys, and football, I've heard gems such as "you shoot an old horse in the face" or "you smash a snake and drink the blood, yes?" Several of the stereotypes about the culture of Rio Grande do Sul were captured in the 2013 film "O Tempo E O Vento" (The Time and the Wind). It was filmed just outside of Bagé on a set called Santa Fe. The film describes the 150-year rivalry between two families living in Rio Grande do Sul. The set is meant to emulate a 17th/18th century village, with homes, stores and other various small buildings. When I arrived, a man dressed in traditional gaúcho clothing (lenço, bombacha, etc.) was picking fruit from a tree in the center of the village courtyard.

"It's a bit sour, but give it a try," he said, tossing me a piece.

"Thank you," I said, and bit in. I grimaced at the taste - he was right to warn me. "Do you work here?"

"If you call it work," he laughed. "I just take care of the grounds, talk to visitors."

"Do you get many?" I ask. "No," is his terse reply.

It didn't help that their hours were "from around 3 to sunset". I happened to be lucky enough to arrive at 4.

"You're from America...come speak English to my daughter!" he said, gesturing to an about 9 year old girl playing with a doll under a nearby tree. This is a common theme - adults are often ashamed to speak English, though most do know some. However, they present their kids as unenthused offerings, saying "Here, help her learn, talk English to her!" While Americans may be cynical about "The American Dream", it is alive and well here. America is seen as a gateway to opportunity, an easy path to being rich and famous. They want their kids to have a better life, and many people see English as the gateway to work for an international company.

I exchange a few sentences with his daughter about her school and her friends, and her father looks very pleased.

"I live just across the field," he said, pointing to a small cabin perched on top of a nearby hill. "Come by one Sunday and I'll teach you how to make a traditional churrasco (barbeque)."

From Club to Conservatory

I probably walked up and down the main street of Bagé a thousand times. I lived on the very north edge, and I would walk down it to get almost everywhere I needed to go - the grocery store, the movies, or my favorite brewery. There was always one building, towards the center of the city, that stood out to me - a gorgeous, ancient, pink building. One day I decided to go inside. As soon as I walked in, a kindly older woman smiled and answered my question before I even had to ask:

"Welcome! This is the Municipal Institute of Fine Arts (IMBA), a music and dance conservatory, and has been for the past 96 years!"

A line of little girls in pink tutus suddenly appeared and dashed down the hallway past us. I looked up in awe at the ornate carvings that decorated the grand entry hall. Amidst the furniture stores and street vendors and plazas of downtown Bagé, this architectural masterpiece was nonchalantly available for the public to explore.

"It's amazing! But the building is even older than that, isn't it?" I asked.

"Oh, yes. It was built in 1868 by the Spanish Society. It used to be a gentlemen's club. But we like it better like this!" she said, laughing.

She gave me the grand tour, showing me all the pianos and introducing me to students and handing out lollipops to everyone for some inexplicable reason. Old portraits of mustachioed gentlemen were hung everywhere. Walking through that building, I felt like I had somehow travelled in both space and time back to 19th century Spain.

"Thank you for showing me this! It is beautiful."

We stood in the doorway, and she kissed me goodbye on both cheeks.

"You deserve it!" she said, and handed me a lollipop.

At the Gym

"Oi, Kur-chee!"

This is how I'm greeted by the owner every time I arrive at the gym. The "t" sound is hard for Brazilians to pronounce, so that's what my name turns in to here. He is a huge, very in-shape and manly guy. So it's even funnier for me that when I leave, he always says "Um Abraço!" This is a typical goodbye in Brazil, but I could never imagine a gym owner in the US saying "A hug!" to another man at the gym.

There are a couple other interesting differences in the gyms of Bagé. For example, there's a shared water cup by the water fountain that everyone uses. No one seems to give a second thought to sharing drinks, or passing germs from using the same straw.

Also, there are often kids running around and people stopping to chat all the time with each other. I would rarely see those things at a gym in America.

Finally, one guy saw an exercise I was doing and asked for help. He said he'd never seen it before and wanted me to show him how to do it!

People are curious as to why an American is in the gym, and will come up and say hello. One day, someone had Googled pictures of their hometown on the beach in the state of São Paulo and was showing them to me.

Unfortunately, when you Google pictures of my hometown, you just get about 20 pictures of a cult compound on fire.

"How was the adjustment to life here?" I asked him, trying to change the subject.

"There's not as much to do here...you make your own fun."

The Bilingual Jokester

"So, a cat is chasing a mouse down a hallway..."

My ears perk up, as the speaker is beginning a joke in Portuguese. I'm always eager to learn more about humor in Brazil, because I think the way people joke is very key to understanding who they are. However, I'm struggling to keep up with the quick back and forth of the group of native speakers.

"The mouse sees a hole in the baseboard, and scurries in to hide. After waiting for a while, the mouse hears a loud bark. 'Aha!' says the mouse. 'The dog will chase the cat away and I will be free!' The mouse waits a bit, then scurries out of the hole. To his dismay, the cat is still there! It pounces on him and is about to bite. 'Hold on, Mr. Cat!" says the mouse. "Ok, ok, you got me, fair and square. But before you eat me, tell me, what happened to the dog?' 'Dog?" says the cat. "There was no dog. In today's economy...who isn't bilingual?'"

The crowd dies laughing. It's a corny joke, but we all love it. Because it's very true, especially in Brazil. Not knowing English can cut you off from job opportunities.

"Where did you hear that joke?" I asked the jokester afterwards.

"New Zealand," he says. " I studied abroad there. It was so hard, going there and barely speaking any English. So many people helped me, showed me the ropes. Now, I have a great job at a big agro-business with soy, rice, and cattle here in Rio Grande do Sul."

"That's amazing that you got to study there," I say. "What do you think that time living there taught you?"

"To be kind to strangers," he responds. "When you go back to America, you'll be the first in your community to help someone who doesn't speak English. You've had this experience. You know what it's like to be a stranger in a strange land. So you help the next guy out! It's that simple."

The Sunday Scaries

For many of us, the "Sunday Scaries" is a real thing that hits us in the waning hours of each weekend.

The worries and dread of the upcoming work week can ruin our final evening of freedom each Sunday night. Here in Bagé, the most common way to dispel them involves the following steps:

1.   Get dressed up and pile into a car with your friends.

2.   Drive to the main street (Sete de Setembro) and park the car, stand around nearby, and leave the music blaring traditional Brazilian "sertanejo" (country) or funk (hip-hop).

3.   Prepare a chimarrão (also known as maté) for your squad, refill the cup constantly, and pass it around continually.

4.   Loiter.

If this sounds like more fun than you can handle, another option is to attend one of the many pentacostal churches that are springing up around the country.

Last night, I showed up at Bolo De Neve (Snowball) Church, a neo-pentacostal organization that has church plants all over the world. The pastor named it this because he heard a word from God saying the church would grow like a snowball rolling down a mountain. He is a surfer with a degree in marketing, so the altar in each church is in the shape of a surfboard.

I was a bit worried at first, because someone told me about the "culto" they have each week. However, I calmed down a bit after finding out this was just the Portuguese word for "worship service". The crowd of about 100 people there was young, full of energy, and I was greeted warmly and shown to a seat as I arrived.

After a few announcements, the church erupted into worship led by a praise band. People were shouting, dancing in the front of the church, and the pastor was blowing a shofar (instrument used by Israelites in Bible times). All the doors were closed and the heat was oppressive, but that didn't hinder any congregants from dancing and shouting despite the sweat.

Finally, the music ended and the pastor got up to speak:

"First of all, raise your hand if you're a visitor! I heard we even have an American in the house."

All eyes turned on me. So much for trying to blend in.

"I don't speak English!" he says in English, much to the chagrin of the crowd, who erupt in applause and laughter.

He then flips back to Portuguese. "But, brother, you can start an English service here. Who would like to go to a service here in English?"

The crowd erupts again in applause and laughter, and dozens of hands go up.

"Don't worry, I'll preach very slowly tonight so you can understand."

The crowd is loving it. My presence has allowed the pastor to flex his comedic muscles, and everyone is eating it up.

Long story short, I eventually snuck out the back after almost 2 hours. The service was still going strong.

The Burger Joint

"Look, the biggest burger is called the American! You'd like that, wouldn't you?"

I'm standing in an industrial burger kitchen, wearing a hairnet, as the owner of FunBurger is showing me his menu. I had met him about an hour ago at an event downtown, and he offered to show me his restaurant. We arrived at one of the nicest houses in town, and walked inside to see a plush living room decorated with fine paintings and furniture. His mother and wife were hanging out and watching a Brazilian soap opera, The Other Side of Paradise. We kept walking past the living room and, we suddenly arrived at a bustling kitchen that closely resembles the back of a fast food restaurant. We washed up, put on our hairnets, and he showed me the grill, the fry cooker, and had me taste the different sauces.

No one is wearing gloves as they prepare the meals, but every thirty minutes they all have to wash their hands. Better than nothing, I guess?

"I went to Pelotas, a two hour drive to the nearest fast food chain restaurant, and studied their process. I bought their old equipment that we use here, and I've worked for 2 years to nail the sauces."

I bit into a big burger. It was incredible.

"The difference here is the meat," he continued. "The quality of beef here in Rio Grande de Sul is unmatched in the world. It's only top notch patties that we serve here."

Afterwards, we sat outside and I sang Coldplay while he played the guitar. Delivery men on motorcycles zoomed in and out (the restaurant is delivery or drive-up only, no sit-down restaurant).

"Tell me something," he asked. "Do Americans really leave the doors to their homes unlocked, like in the movies?"

"It depends," I say. "Some do in suburban neighborhoods that are pretty safe. But if you don't live in an area like that, probably not."

"I couldn't even imagine leaving a door unlocked," he responds, shaking his head. "It's like you lived in a whole different world!"

The Weekly Thud

"It's been a very long time since I spoke any English!"

He is closing the windows after rehearsal, and bashfully not making any eye contact as we speak. This is the kind of quality person who he is – he knows it may rain later tonight, so he's taken it on himself to do this to protect the classroom when everyone else has gone home.

"When was the last time?" I ask.

"I was studying physics in New York for one year. Must have been almost 20 years ago now."

"Did you like living there?"

"I was researching and working all the time so I didn't see much of it. And my English was very bad so it was hard to meet people."

"Your English is still pretty good now after all these years!"

"Oh, no..." he says, modestly. This is a common trend that I've found. People who speak fairly good English are ashamed when speaking with a native speaker, and get embarrassed because they feel they are messing up often. I know I make many more errors when I'm speaking Portuguese than they do when speaking English!

The choir at the local university is called "Baque do Pampa", which roughly translated, means "the thump of the grasslands". The Pampas are a grassy region that encompasses northern Argentina, Uruguay, and the south of Brazil.

We are a group of all ages and all skill levels, open to anyone in the local community. We meet every Wednesday for two hours and sing our hearts out. It is delightful.

The first half an hour or so of each rehearsal is teaching fundamentals of singing – breath support, warm ups, etc. Brazilian culture is much more comfortable with touching than American culture, so our professora puts her hand on everyone's stomach in turn to test how our breathing is going. She laughed when I flinched the first time this happened, unused to this sort of contact.

This week, when we were practicing breathing (in for 5 seconds, holding our breath for 5 seconds, then out for 5 seconds) an older woman next to me jabbed me lightly in the stomach with her elbow in the middle of the "holding our breath" part.

Surprised, I exhaled loudly when I was not supposed to, and was scolded good-naturedly by our choir teacher. The woman next to me, who couldn't have been an inch taller than 5 feet, laughed her head off. I couldn't help but laugh too.

As the only native English speaker in the choir, I was called to the front this week to help with pronunciation of the 1965 hit from The Mamas and The Papas, "California Dreamin' ".

Having 50 Brazilians, many of whom know almost no English, repeat each phrase of the lyrics after you is quite an experience. And trying to explain the meaning of the line "on such a winter's day" in Portuguese proved difficult.

But on and on we sing. In Portuguese, English, and even Zulu, our repertoire spans genres and eras. And no matter what language we sing or where we come from, we all sing with gusto because our weekly "thud" sessions bring us joy.

The Devout Mathematician

"So I sat in the pew, looked at the cross, and asked if He was crazy, a liar, or the real thing. And, just like that, I decided to come back to the church."

We've just finished band practice for Codigo de Barras ("The Bar Codes"), where he is the drummer and I am filling in as temporary lead singer. We meet in his garage every Friday afternoon, and do everything from 2000s US alternative to modern Brazilian rock. He is packing up the drumsticks as his little daughter hops up in his lap.

"But haven't you always been Catholic?" I asked.

"Yes, just like everyone in Brazil. But, after I heard the answer to that question, I decided to do it for real."

"How do you feel like your faith interacts with your work as a math professor?"

"Math is what God uses to talk to us! This chair, that TV, the cells in your own body. Math is everywhere, and it is certain, and it is how He lets us know that He is real."

"Do you ever have doubts?"

"Of course. Like my priest says - faith and doubt always walk together. You just have to decide if you want to be a believer struggling with doubt or a doubter struggling with belief. I think the former makes more sense, and will give you a happier life!"

"What do your colleagues think when you talk about math and faith together?"

"I did my P.H.D. in Portugal, and even got to present my dissertation at Oxford. I was blessed to be around really smart people. But ever since I've come back to the church, I understand that I am rare in my field."

"How so? Most mathematicians are atheist, right?"

"Yes, but even those who believe in God often see it as a tradeoff. But I don't. My love of logic makes me believe even more deeply in the divine."

The Dinner Party

Sometimes, responding to a random Facebook message from a stranger might give your computer a virus. But other times, it will give you an opportunity to have a home-cooked meal and chat by a fire with a lovely family.

Thankfully, my experience one Friday night was the latter. I received a message inviting me over to dinner, and having checked with our mutual friends to make sure he was reputable, I was welcomed into his family's home to a dinner of "Crazy Hair Chicken" (the rough English translation, the "hair" was potato slices), lasagna, and plenty of olive oil.

"Both our grandparents came here from Italy, so these are the kind of dishes we were raised eating," his wife said as she served me a generous portion.

"We're so glad you could come over. We love welcoming guests, and practicing English!" he said.

"I make better grades in English than in Portuguese!" laughed his daughter, a sophomore at a local private school.

"What inspires you all to learn the language?" I asked.

"Music!" his daughter said, without hesitation. "I'm in love with Shawn Mendes and his songs are all in English. If you want to sing any popular songs, you have to be able to understand it."

"Learning new things," responds his wife. "We watch educational videos on YouTube, and there's an American nutritionist I love who teaches me a lot of great things."

"I used to live in America," he responds. "I worked at a farm outside of Alexandria, Virginia for four months. I practiced English every day for five years before I went, and I loved it there. Ever since I've been trying to improve. I'm a soy and rice farmer, and I went to Nebraska for a conference a few years ago and did a road trip around the Midwest. It is so beautiful, and the roads are so good! If I lived in America, I would be road tripping everywhere."

After dinner, their daughter went to bed and I sat by the fire with the couple. We shared a bottle of really good local wine.

"Did you have any funny stories about learning the language? I know I have a ton from learning Portuguese."

"Yes! One time, I was the only person home when the mailman came. He went to the wrong door, and I was trying to tell him to 'go around' so I could open the main door. But instead I said 'turn around'! Puzzled, he did a 360 degree spin for me. Then he asked, 'Now can I give you your mail?'"

We all died laughing.

"What do you hope for Brazil in the future? Or Bagé in particular?"

"Lots of things." she said. "But the one that comes to mind most is doing a better job caring for our past. There's not a culture of preserving history here. It's really a shame. We had so many beautiful buildings, and now they are just falling apart. Future generations will not be able to appreciate the stories of Bagé."

"She's right," he said. "And also for people to focus on what's important. Right now the World Cup is great, and we're doing well, which is good. But people don't plan for the long term here, we just live in the present too much. There are so many things that we need to improve, and things like sports can just be distractions."

The Expat Club

"Our players are humble and they work like crazy! That's why we win."

The light blue building in downtown Bagé is full of mostly older men, drinking beer and smoking cigarettes. This is the Sociedade Uruguaia de Socorros Mútuos em Bagé, otherwise known as the expat club for Uruguays who live here in this small Brazilian town 60 kilometers north of the border with their home country. The man I'm talking to is speaking Spanish, as is everyone else in the club, and I'm having a hard time discerning the meaning. But from what I can understand, he is saying:

"One of our players was almost starving when he started playing club soccer, he used to get an extra meal whenever he scored a goal."

"And how many times have y'all won the World Cup?" I ask.

"Twice. 1930 and 1950. And we had a population of about 2 million then. We are by far the smallest county to ever win."

"In what ways is Uruguay different from this part of Brazil?"

"In many ways the same. The language I would say is the biggest difference, here on the other side of the border. But we are all gauchos, we drink mate and make a hard living working with our hands – raising cows, growing rice, and things like that."

We're currently watching Uruguay take on the powerhouse Portugal, and the game is tied 1-1. One older gentleman has a drum that he continually plays when Uruguay is on the offense.

"That drum is part of Candombe, a traditional Uruguayan music. We had a big show last Friday night with some of the best players."

He's cut off from continuing because the crowd is going wild. Uruguay has just scored and everyone is jumping up and down, waving flags, raising beers.

A few more minutes and the game is over. Uruguay has advanced to the next round!

HONÓRIO LEMES

The English Enthusiast

"I'm a Mormon-hunter, you know," he says, casually. "Excuse me?" I reply, almost spitting out my drink.

We are sound checking on the stage of the Los Angeles Pub, and I am testing the microphone while he plugs in his acoustic guitar.

"About 5 years ago, I was in Santa Maria waiting for the bus to come back to Bagé. I had just finished visiting family, and I was thinking about how I could improve my English. I've always loved the language, but I wanted to improve my accent and talk to native speakers. I had just started my English school here in Bagé, and I wanted to have native speakers to help me record my curriculum. But we only get them once in a blue moon around here."

"But the Mormons, man, you gotta explain that..."

"Yes, yes! So, I was sitting there waiting, when all of the sudden a huge crowd of young Mormons came to the bus station. I learned later on that they had their regional training there in Santa Maria, and were being sent out to all the small towns of Rio Grande do Sol. I heard them all speaking English, and I got so excited. I boarded my bus and was waiting for some of them to get on, but they kept boarding other buses. At the last minute, right before our bus pulled away, two of them got on!"

"How did you get to know them?"

"Well, I actually became Mormon for a while. I know it sounds bad, but it was because I wanted to practice English with them. Every time Mormons have come to Bagé, I have become their friends. But these were great guys, especially the first two. One of them invited me to his wedding in Utah. I couldn't go obviously, but I still use the save-the-date to teach about American culture."

"Did it ever feel fake? Like you were using each other in some way – them, to try to convert you, and you, to try to learn English?"

"I get that, definitely. It is an odd relationship. There is that sense, at the beginning, of ulterior motives. But each time it has blossomed into honest friendships. Looking back now, I think religion is bad but people are good. What's important is that we were developing real relationships with people that think and believe differently from each other, all while enjoying life."

The Wry Banker

"If you survive August, you live another year."

Delivered like an ancient proverb, the speaker pulls out two 1 Real coins from his pocket and trades me for a 2 Real bill.

"That's really what they say around here about the cold?" I ask. I hadn't brought any winter clothes, thinking that Brazil would be hot year round. However, Bagé is one of the coldest cities in the whole country, and very few buildings have central heat. Many nights in July, I would lay huddled in bed as the temperature dipped down to 40 degrees Fahrenheit.

"Yep. It's true, you just have to make it through this month. Then it gets better."

To explain our transaction, the local movie theater gives a discount if you pay in all 1 Real coins. Since we had nothing better to do that morning, we were going around local businesses trying to trade in 5 or 2 Real bills for 1 Real coins. And it was surprisingly tougher than we expected.

"Coin? Coin is difficult," was the cryptic response of almost everyone we asked, paired with a startled and wary look on their faces. This included the cashier at the restaurant I was currently standing in.

Thankfully, my didactic, coin-toting friend who was waiting in line to pay could explain this mystery.

"I'm a banker here, and we have so much difficulty keeping enough coins flowing through circulation. You see, more coins are very rarely printed, so there is a finite supply here in Bagé. And there is a custom here of saving coins throughout the year in a piggy bank whenever you get them."

"And what are they used for?"

"Around December, people take their saved coins and spend it all on vacation during Christmas and the New Year."

"They show up to your bank to cash in, with just huge stashes full of all kinds of coins?"

"Sometimes. It's pretty silly if you think about it, there are so many better ways to save money. However, it's the way people in Bagé have been saving for generations. So, yeah, around August and September the coin supply begins to dry up. And don't even think about finding a coin in November."

"Thanks!" I say, wincing as I open the door and am slapped with the icy wind.

The banker raises his coffee cup to me and offers as a goodbye, "Here's to surviving!"

Unsettled by his parting toast, I leave the restaurant and hurry to the theater. This final swap has given me the last two coins I needed for the movie! As I walk outside, I am again struck by how odd it is to see cars and horse-drawn carts sharing the streets peacefully.

But, as luck would have it, the theater was closed. No explanation, just "Cancelled" posted outside, even though their website said the movie was playing.

Oh, well. I shoved my hands in my pockets and felt the jangle of the fruits of my labors. At least I'd have some coins for November.

The Brazilian Moon

"You know we've got some moon here, don't you?"

I'm talking to the curator of the Dom Diogo de Souza Museum, an imposing nineteenth-century building nestled in the heart of Bagé. She dropped this curious fact on me out of nowhere, after exchanging a few pleasantries and welcoming me to the local history museum.

"No way!" I reply. "How did you get it?"

"The last time a human was on the moon was 1972. As a part of the Apollo 17 mission that year, astronaut Harrison Schmitt collected hundreds of rocks from the moon to be given as a commemorative goodwill offering to all the countries of the world. U.S. President Nixon presented a plaque display containing the moon fragment to Brazilian President Medici, who was a native of Bagé. And he donated it to us!"

"Amazing! How big is it?"

"It's tiny!" she says, using her fingers to show me. "Only a centimeter and a half across. But it is a source of pride for Bagé."

"Can I see it?"

"Sorry, but no. We've only exhibited it a handful of times over the past 30 something years - we keep it in a secure vault."

As they should - one estimate values the piece at over $10 million USD!

Good Energy

After eight months, it was my last night in Bagé. I was strolling down the main street, and I was suddenly sad to be leaving. I'd been counting down the days until I could escape just yesterday, but somehow, today, everything was so special. Suddenly, I knew this strange dreamlike year would end, of drinking chimmarão, of being a local celebrity, of wandering through a remarkable town.

I went to my favorite brewery and bakery one last time to say goodbye to our friends. I then went to hang out with one of my best friends at the university who was from Cape Verde, making him one of the only other non-South Americans in town. We went to sit in plastic chairs outside the gas station, a classic spot where we used to hang out and watch the cars come down the street. And he decided to leave me with some parting wisdom.

"People have good and bad energy. If you're around those with bad energy too much, it sucks the life out of you. You become poisoned by it, if you let yourself become too close to someone with this draining energy. So, surround yourself with people with good energy. Happy, positive people. That will transfer unto you. That's why we are friends."

I started crying softly, taking hard sips from a cold beer can.

"Don't worry, we will see each other again, I know," he said. "You are welcome in my home in Cape Verde, anytime. You can stay with my family."

I gave him a long hug, slapped on the back a few times, as men do, and he left me at my sad, lonely door. I don't know if I'll ever see him again. But I wish him well. I send him good energy, all the way from Texas, wherever he is now. It makes me so damn sad to think about that year being gone. Every single chance encounter there was holy and unbelievable and precious.

A wise person once told me: "Anything can be interesting, if you pay enough attention." A town that many of its own residents dismiss as boring, I found beautiful and charming and intensely fascinating.

And that was the end of a curious and strange year marooned where the devil lost his boots. I'm already forgetting many of the facts, but I will never forget the way it made me feel. So many characters, larger than life, loom in my head as I try to fall asleep at night. And I know that thinking back on their lives, their stories, and their home will bring me good energy for the rest of my life.

www.ingramcontent.com/pod-product-compliance
Lightning Source LLC
Chambersburg PA
CBHW040711150426

42811CB00061B/1819